1		
2		
3		
4		
5		
6		
7		
8		
9		
10		
11		
12		
13		
14		
15		
16		
17		
18		
19		
20		

21		
22		
23		
24		
25		
26		
27		
28		
29		
30		
31		
32		
33		
34		
35		
36		
37		
38		
39		
40		

41		
42		
43		
44		
45		
46		
47		
48		
49		
50		
51		
52		
53		
54		
55		
56		
57		
58		
59		
60		

61		
62		
63		
64		
65		
66		
67		
68		
69		
70		
71		
72		
73		
74		
75		
76		
77		
78		
79		
80		

81		
82		
83		
84		
85		
86		
87		
88		
89		
90		
91		
92		
93		
94		
95		
96		
97		
98		
99		
100		

Book Title

Author | Nationality

Genre | Year | Pages

Memorable Quote	Page Number

Characters

Plot Summary

Notes

Rating ☆ ☆ ☆ ☆ ☆

Book Title

Author

Nationality

Genre

Year

Pages

Memorable Quote	Page Number

Characters

Plot Summary

Notes

Rating ☆ ☆ ☆ ☆ ☆

Book Title ______________________

Author ______________________ Nationality ______________________

Genre ______________________ Year ______________________ Pages ______________________

Memorable Quote	Page Number

Characters

Plot Summary

Notes

Rating ☆ ☆ ☆ ☆ ☆

Book Title

Author

Nationality

Genre

Year

Pages

Memorable Quote	Page Number

Characters

Plot Summary

Notes

Rating ☆ ☆ ☆ ☆ ☆

Book Title 5

Author

Nationality

Genre

Year

Pages

Memorable Quote	Page Number

Characters

Plot Summary

Notes

Rating ☆ ☆ ☆ ☆ ☆

Book Title

Author

Nationality

Genre

Year

Pages

Memorable Quote	Page Number

Characters

Plot Summary

Notes

Rating ☆ ☆ ☆ ☆ ☆

Book Title

Author Nationality

Genre Year Pages

Memorable Quote	Page Number

Characters

Plot Summary

Notes

Rating ☆ ☆ ☆ ☆ ☆

Book Title ______________________

Author ______________________ Nationality ______________________

Genre ______________________ Year ______________________ Pages __________

Memorable Quote	Page Number

Characters

Plot Summary

Notes

Rating ☆ ☆ ☆ ☆ ☆

Book Title ______________________

Author ______________________ Nationality ______________________

Genre ______________________ Year ______________________ Pages __________

Memorable Quote	Page Number

Characters

Plot Summary

Notes

Rating ☆ ☆ ☆ ☆ ☆

Book Title

Author

Nationality

Genre

Year

Pages

Memorable Quote	Page Number

Characters

Plot Summary

Notes

Rating ☆ ☆ ☆ ☆ ☆

Book Title

Author ______ Nationality ______

Genre ______ Year ______ Pages ______

Memorable Quote	Page Number

Characters

Plot Summary

Notes

Rating ☆ ☆ ☆ ☆ ☆

Book Title

Author Nationality

Genre Year Pages

Memorable Quote	Page Number

Characters

Plot Summary

Notes

Rating ☆ ☆ ☆ ☆ ☆

Book Title ______________________

Author ______________ Nationality ______________

Genre ______________ Year ______________ Pages ______________

Memorable Quote	Page Number

Characters

Plot Summary

Notes

Rating ☆ ☆ ☆ ☆ ☆

Book Title

Author

Nationality

Genre

Year

Pages

Memorable Quote	Page Number

Characters

Plot Summary

Notes

Rating ☆ ☆ ☆ ☆ ☆

Book Title ______________________ 15

Author ______________ Nationality ______________

Genre ______________ Year ______________ Pages ________

Memorable Quote	Page Number

Characters

Plot Summary

Notes

Rating ☆ ☆ ☆ ☆ ☆

Book Title

Author 	Nationality

Genre 	Year 	Pages

Memorable Quote	Page Number

Characters

Plot Summary

Notes

Rating ☆ ☆ ☆ ☆ ☆

Book Title

Author

Nationality

Genre

Year

Pages

Memorable Quote	Page Number

Characters

Plot Summary

Notes

Rating ☆ ☆ ☆ ☆ ☆

18

Book Title

Author

Nationality

Genre

Year

Pages

Memorable Quote	Page Number

Characters

Plot Summary

Notes

Rating ☆ ☆ ☆ ☆ ☆

19

Book Title

Author ______________________ Nationality ______________________

Genre ______________________ Year ______________________ Pages __________

Memorable Quote	Page Number

Characters

Plot Summary

Notes

Rating

Book Title ______________________

Author ______________ Nationality ______________

Genre ______________ Year ______________ Pages ________

Memorable Quote	Page Number

Characters

Plot Summary

Notes

Rating ☆ ☆ ☆ ☆ ☆

Book Title ____________________

Author ____________________ Nationality ____________________

Genre ____________________ Year ____________________ Pages ____________________

Memorable Quote	Page Number

Characters

Plot Summary

Notes

Rating ☆ ☆ ☆ ☆ ☆

Book Title

Author

Nationality

Genre

Year

Pages

Memorable Quote	Page Number

Characters

Plot Summary

Notes

Rating ☆ ☆ ☆ ☆ ☆

Book Title

Author

Nationality

Genre

Year

Pages

Memorable Quote	Page Number

Characters

Plot Summary

Notes

Rating ☆ ☆ ☆ ☆ ☆

24

Book Title

Author

Nationality

Genre

Year

Pages

Memorable Quote	Page Number

Characters

Plot Summary

Notes

Rating ☆ ☆ ☆ ☆ ☆

Book Title

Author

Nationality

Genre

Year

Pages

Memorable Quote	Page Number

Characters

Plot Summary

Notes

Rating ☆ ☆ ☆ ☆ ☆

Book Title

Author Nationality

Genre Year Pages

Memorable Quote	Page Number

Characters

Plot Summary

Notes

Rating ☆ ☆ ☆ ☆ ☆

27

Book Title

Author Nationality

Genre Year Pages

Memorable Quote	Page Number

Characters

Plot Summary

Notes

Rating ☆ ☆ ☆ ☆ ☆

28

Book Title

Author

Nationality

Genre

Year

Pages

Memorable Quote	Page Number

Characters

Plot Summary

Notes

Rating ☆ ☆ ☆ ☆ ☆

29

Book Title ______________________

Author ______________ Nationality ______________

Genre ______________ Year ______________ Pages ______

Memorable Quote	Page Number

Characters

Plot Summary

Notes

Rating ☆ ☆ ☆ ☆ ☆

30

Book Title

Author

Nationality

Genre

Year

Pages

Memorable Quote	Page Number

Characters

Plot Summary

Notes

Rating ☆ ☆ ☆ ☆ ☆

Book Title ______________________

Author ______________________ Nationality ______________________

Genre ______________________ Year ______________________ Pages ______________________

Memorable Quote	Page Number

Characters

Plot Summary

Notes

Rating ☆ ☆ ☆ ☆ ☆

32

Book Title

Author

Nationality

Genre

Year

Pages

Memorable Quote	Page Number

Characters

Plot Summary

Notes

Rating ☆ ☆ ☆ ☆ ☆

33

Book Title ____________________

Author ____________________ Nationality ____________________

Genre ____________________ Year ____________________ Pages __________

Memorable Quote	Page Number

Characters

Plot Summary

Notes

Rating ☆ ☆ ☆ ☆ ☆

34

Book Title

Author | Nationality

Genre | Year | Pages

Memorable Quote	Page Number

Characters

Plot Summary

Notes

Rating ☆ ☆ ☆ ☆ ☆

Book Title

Author ____________ Nationality ____________

Genre ____________ Year ____________ Pages ____________

Memorable Quote	Page Number

Characters

Plot Summary

Notes

Rating ☆ ☆ ☆ ☆ ☆

36

Book Title

Author

Nationality

Genre

Year

Pages

Memorable Quote	Page Number

Characters

Plot Summary

Notes

Rating ☆ ☆ ☆ ☆ ☆

37

Book Title

Author

Nationality

Genre

Year

Pages

Memorable Quote	Page Number

Characters

Plot Summary

Notes

Rating ☆ ☆ ☆ ☆ ☆

38

Book Title

Author

Nationality

Genre

Year

Pages

Memorable Quote	Page Number

Characters

Plot Summary

Notes

Rating ☆ ☆ ☆ ☆ ☆

39

Book Title

Author

Nationality

Genre

Year

Pages

Memorable Quote	Page Number

Characters

Plot Summary

Notes

Rating ☆ ☆ ☆ ☆ ☆

40

Book Title

Author

Nationality

Genre

Year

Pages

Memorable Quote	Page Number

Characters

Plot Summary

Notes

Rating ☆ ☆ ☆ ☆ ☆

41

Book Title ____________________

Author ____________________ Nationality ____________________

Genre ____________________ Year ____________________ Pages __________

Memorable Quote	Page Number

Characters

Plot Summary

Notes

Rating ☆ ☆ ☆ ☆ ☆

42

Book Title

Author

Nationality

Genre

Year

Pages

Memorable Quote	Page Number

Characters

Plot Summary

Notes

Rating ☆ ☆ ☆ ☆ ☆

Book Title ____________________

Author ____________________ Nationality ____________________

Genre ____________________ Year ____________________ Pages __________

Memorable Quote	Page Number

Characters

Plot Summary

Notes

Rating ☆ ☆ ☆ ☆ ☆

44

Book Title

Author Nationality

Genre Year Pages

Memorable Quote	Page Number

Characters

Plot Summary

Notes

Rating ☆ ☆ ☆ ☆ ☆

45

Book Title ____________________

Author ____________________ Nationality ____________________

Genre ____________________ Year ____________________ Pages __________

Memorable Quote	Page Number

Characters

Plot Summary

Notes

Rating ☆ ☆ ☆ ☆ ☆

Book Title

Author

Nationality

Genre

Year

Pages

46

Memorable Quote	Page Number

Characters

Plot Summary

Notes

Rating ☆ ☆ ☆ ☆ ☆

Book Title

Author

Nationality

Genre

Year

Pages

Memorable Quote	Page Number

Characters

Plot Summary

Notes

Rating ☆ ☆ ☆ ☆ ☆

Book Title ______________________

Author ______________________ Nationality ______________________

Genre ______________________ Year ______________________ Pages ____________

Memorable Quote	Page Number

Characters

Plot Summary

Notes

Rating ☆ ☆ ☆ ☆ ☆

Book Title ______________________

49

Author ______________ Nationality ______________

Genre ______________ Year ______________ Pages ______

Memorable Quote	Page Number

Characters

Plot Summary

Notes

Rating ☆ ☆ ☆ ☆ ☆

50

Book Title ______________________

Author ______________________ Nationality ______________________

Genre ______________________ Year ______________________ Pages ____________

Memorable Quote	Page Number

Characters

Plot Summary

Notes

Rating ☆ ☆ ☆ ☆ ☆

51

Book Title

Author ______________________ Nationality ______________

Genre ______________________ Year ______________ Pages ________

Memorable Quote	Page Number

Characters

Plot Summary

Notes

Rating ☆ ☆ ☆ ☆ ☆

52

Book Title ______________________

Author ______________________ Nationality ______________________

Genre ______________________ Year ______________________ Pages ______________________

Memorable Quote	Page Number

Characters

Plot Summary

Notes

Rating ☆ ☆ ☆ ☆ ☆

Book Title

Author

Nationality

Genre

Year

Pages

Memorable Quote	Page Number

Characters

Plot Summary

Notes

Rating ☆ ☆ ☆ ☆ ☆

Book Title

Author

Nationality

Genre

Year

Pages

54

Memorable Quote	Page Number

Characters

Plot Summary

Notes

Rating ☆ ☆ ☆ ☆ ☆

Book Title

Author ______________________ Nationality ______________________

Genre ______________________ Year ______________________ Pages ____________

Memorable Quote	Page Number

Characters

Plot Summary

Notes

Rating ☆ ☆ ☆ ☆ ☆

Book Title

Author

Nationality

Genre

Year

Pages

Memorable Quote	Page Number

Characters

Plot Summary

Notes

Rating ☆ ☆ ☆ ☆ ☆

Book Title

57

Author

Nationality

Genre

Year

Pages

Memorable Quote	Page Number

Characters

Plot Summary

Notes

Rating ☆ ☆ ☆ ☆ ☆

Book Title

Author

Nationality

Genre

Year

Pages

Memorable Quote	Page Number

Characters

Plot Summary

Notes

Rating ☆ ☆ ☆ ☆ ☆

Book Title

Author

Nationality

Genre

Year

Pages

Memorable Quote	Page Number

Characters

Plot Summary

Notes

Rating ☆ ☆ ☆ ☆ ☆

Book Title

Author

Nationality

Genre

Year

Pages

Memorable Quote	Page Number

Characters

Plot Summary

Notes

Rating ☆ ☆ ☆ ☆ ☆

61

Book Title

Author

Nationality

Genre

Year

Pages

Memorable Quote	Page Number

Characters

Plot Summary

Notes

Rating ☆ ☆ ☆ ☆ ☆

Book Title

Author

Nationality

Genre

Year

Pages

Memorable Quote	Page Number

Characters

Plot Summary

Notes

Rating ☆ ☆ ☆ ☆ ☆

Book Title

Author ______ Nationality ______

Genre ______ Year ______ Pages ______

Memorable Quote	Page Number

Characters

Plot Summary

Notes

Rating ☆ ☆ ☆ ☆ ☆

64

Book Title

Author

Nationality

Genre

Year

Pages

Memorable Quote	Page Number

Characters

Plot Summary

Notes

Rating ☆ ☆ ☆ ☆ ☆

Book Title

Author

Nationality

Genre

Year

Pages

Memorable Quote	Page Number

Characters

Plot Summary

Notes

Rating ☆ ☆ ☆ ☆ ☆

Book Title

Author

Nationality

Genre

Year

Pages

Memorable Quote	Page Number

Characters

Plot Summary

Notes

Rating ☆ ☆ ☆ ☆ ☆

67

Book Title

Author

Nationality

Genre

Year

Pages

Memorable Quote	Page Number

Characters

Plot Summary

Notes

Rating ☆ ☆ ☆ ☆ ☆

Book Title

68

Author

Nationality

Genre

Year

Pages

Memorable Quote	Page Number

Characters

Plot Summary

Notes

Rating ☆ ☆ ☆ ☆ ☆

69

Book Title

Author ______________________ Nationality ______________________

Genre ______________________ Year ______________________ Pages ____________

Memorable Quote	Page Number

Characters

Plot Summary

Notes

Rating ☆ ☆ ☆ ☆ ☆

Book Title

Author

Nationality

Genre

Year

Pages

Memorable Quote	Page Number

Characters

Plot Summary

Notes

Rating ☆ ☆ ☆ ☆ ☆

71

Book Title

Author ______ Nationality ______

Genre ______ Year ______ Pages ______

Memorable Quote	Page Number

Characters

Plot Summary

Notes

Rating ☆ ☆ ☆ ☆ ☆

Book Title ______________________

Author ______________________ Nationality ______________________

Genre ______________________ Year ______________________ Pages ____________

Memorable Quote	Page Number

Characters

Plot Summary

Notes

Rating ☆ ☆ ☆ ☆ ☆

Book Title

73

Author | Nationality

Genre | Year | Pages

Memorable Quote	Page Number

Characters

Plot Summary

Notes

Rating ☆ ☆ ☆ ☆ ☆

Book Title ______

Author ______ Nationality ______

Genre ______ Year ______ Pages ______

74

Memorable Quote	Page Number

Characters

Plot Summary

Notes

Rating ☆ ☆ ☆ ☆ ☆

Book Title

Author

Nationality

Genre

Year

Pages

Memorable Quote	Page Number

Characters

Plot Summary

Notes

Rating ☆ ☆ ☆ ☆ ☆

Book Title

Author ____________ Nationality ____________

Genre ____________ Year ____________ Pages ____________

Memorable Quote	Page Number

Characters

Plot Summary

Notes

Rating ☆ ☆ ☆ ☆ ☆

Book Title

Author ______ Nationality ______

Genre ______ Year ______ Pages ______

Memorable Quote	Page Number

Characters

Plot Summary

Notes

Rating ☆ ☆ ☆ ☆ ☆

Book Title ______________________

Author ______________ Nationality ______________

Genre ______________ Year ______________ Pages ______

78

Memorable Quote	Page Number

Characters

Plot Summary

Notes

Rating ☆ ☆ ☆ ☆ ☆

79

Book Title

Author ____________________ Nationality ____________________

Genre ____________________ Year ____________________ Pages __________

Memorable Quote	Page Number

Characters

Plot Summary

Notes

Rating ☆ ☆ ☆ ☆ ☆

Book Title

80

Author

Nationality

Genre

Year

Pages

Memorable Quote	Page Number

Characters

Plot Summary

Notes

Rating ☆ ☆ ☆ ☆ ☆

81

Book Title

Author

Nationality

Genre

Year

Pages

Memorable Quote	Page Number

Characters

Plot Summary

Notes

Rating ☆ ☆ ☆ ☆ ☆

Book Title

Author

Nationality

Genre

Year

Pages

Memorable Quote	Page Number

Characters

Plot Summary

Notes

Rating ☆ ☆ ☆ ☆ ☆

83

Book Title

Author

Nationality

Genre

Year

Pages

Memorable Quote	Page Number

Characters

Plot Summary

Notes

Rating ☆ ☆ ☆ ☆ ☆

Book Title ____________________

Author ____________________ Nationality ____________________

Genre ____________________ Year ____________________ Pages ____________

Memorable Quote	Page Number

Characters

Plot Summary

Notes

Rating ☆ ☆ ☆ ☆ ☆

Book Title

Author

Nationality

Genre

Year

Pages

Memorable Quote	Page Number

Characters

Plot Summary

Notes

Rating ☆ ☆ ☆ ☆ ☆

86

Book Title ______________________

Author ______________________ Nationality ______________________

Genre ______________________ Year ______________________ Pages ____________

Memorable Quote	Page Number

Characters

Plot Summary

Notes

Rating ☆ ☆ ☆ ☆ ☆

Book Title ______________________

Author ______________________ Nationality ______________________

Genre ______________________ Year ______________________ Pages ______________________

87

Memorable Quote	Page Number

Characters

Plot Summary

Notes

Rating ☆ ☆ ☆ ☆ ☆

Book Title

Author

Nationality

Genre

Year

Pages

Memorable Quote	Page Number

Characters

Plot Summary

Notes

Rating ☆ ☆ ☆ ☆ ☆

Book Title

Author

Nationality

Genre

Year

Pages

Memorable Quote	Page Number

Characters

Plot Summary

Notes

Rating ☆ ☆ ☆ ☆ ☆

Book Title ______________________

Author ______________________ Nationality ______________________

Genre ______________________ Year ______________________ Pages ____________

Memorable Quote	Page Number

Characters

Plot Summary

Notes

Rating ☆ ☆ ☆ ☆ ☆

91

Book Title

Author

Nationality

Genre

Year

Pages

Memorable Quote	Page Number

Characters

Plot Summary

Notes

Rating ☆ ☆ ☆ ☆ ☆

Book Title

Author

Nationality

Genre

Year

Pages

Memorable Quote	Page Number

Characters

Plot Summary

Notes

Rating ☆ ☆ ☆ ☆ ☆

Book Title

Author

Nationality

Genre

Year

Pages

Memorable Quote	Page Number

Characters

Plot Summary

Notes

Rating ☆ ☆ ☆ ☆ ☆

Book Title ____________________

Author ____________________ Nationality ____________________

Genre ____________________ Year ____________________ Pages ____________________

Memorable Quote	Page Number

Characters

Plot Summary

Notes

Rating ☆ ☆ ☆ ☆ ☆

95

Book Title

Author

Nationality

Genre

Year

Pages

Memorable Quote	Page Number

Characters

Plot Summary

Notes

Rating ☆ ☆ ☆ ☆ ☆

Book Title

Author

Nationality

Genre

Year

Pages

Memorable Quote	Page Number

Characters

Plot Summary

Notes

Rating ☆ ☆ ☆ ☆ ☆

Book Title

Author

Nationality

Genre

Year

Pages

Memorable Quote	Page Number

Characters

Plot Summary

Notes

Rating ☆ ☆ ☆ ☆ ☆

98

Book Title ____________________

Author ____________________ Nationality ____________________

Genre ____________________ Year ____________________ Pages ____________

Memorable Quote	Page Number

Characters

Plot Summary

Notes

Rating ☆ ☆ ☆ ☆ ☆

Book Title

Author ______ Nationality ______

Genre ______ Year ______ Pages ______

Memorable Quote	Page Number

Characters

Plot Summary

Notes

Rating ☆ ☆ ☆ ☆ ☆

Book Title ______________________

Author ______________________ Nationality ______________________

Genre ______________________ Year ______________________ Pages ____________

Memorable Quote	Page Number

Characters

Plot Summary

Notes

Rating ☆ ☆ ☆ ☆ ☆

43482280R00059

Made in the USA
Lexington, KY
28 June 2019